How to Overcome Addiction

METROPOLITAN YOUSSEF

Edited and translated by

St. Mary and St. Moses Abbey

How to Overcome Addiction
By Metropolitan Youssef

Designed & Published by:
St. Mary & St. Moses Abbey Press
101 S Vista Dr, Sandia, TX 78383
stmabbeypress.com

Contents

Introduction

When we speak about addiction, the first thing that comes to mind is drug and alcohol addiction because this problem, which floats on the surface, represents a danger threatening individuals, families, and society at large. Therefore, all efforts are focused in the first place on fighting this deadly monster.

Addiction, however, is not in reality limited to only drugs and alcohol, but its concept extends to encompass every habit that holds a person captive. There are two types of addiction: the first is substance addiction, like alcohol addiction, addiction to narcotics, and addiction to some drugs; and the second type is addiction to some habits that control and exercise dominion over a person, like gambling addiction, computer addiction, and so on. The person who is addicted to gambling goes to the gambling places against his will because he is weak-willed, and there he spends countless hours and loses an immense amount of money; nevertheless, he is unable to get rid of this habit. This also applies to computer addiction, which we will address in detail later.

Despite the damage resulting from the dominion of these habits over a person—whether from the health, mental, or material aspect, or their effect on the social condition—nevertheless, the person continues to practice them because he is robbed of his will and freedom.

1

What is Addiction?

Scientists say that substance addiction is essentially a physical dependence, but habit addiction is basically a psychological dependence. For the person feels that he needs to practice this habit because it gives him a sort of satisfaction. The truth, however, is that habit addiction is not completely psychologically dependent but rather has a physical portion also. Likewise, with respect to substance addiction, it is not completely physically dependent but rather has a psychological component also. Researchers have discovered that some habits help the brain release a substance called Beta Endorphin, and it is this that gives a person the feeling of pleasure. And since it is, undoubtedly, a transient feeling, the person, therefore, becomes addicted to the substance which his brain releases. It is true that he does not take an external substance like nicotine or drugs, but he becomes addicted to this substance, which the brain releases. For this reason, he continues to repeat these harmful behaviors because he needs this feeling of pleasure or happiness.

The same thing is thought about physical dependence also. For they found that there was a psychological factor too. The people who have abstained from smoking or drinking alcohol for many years, and then it happened that they went back to it again, a strong desire is found in them to smoke or to drink alcohol. And this desire is a kind of psychological dependence or psychological habituation.

What makes a person repeat a particular habit until he becomes addicted to it is the presence of stress within this person, which compels him to repeat this habit or that behavior, so that he may eliminate the stress that is present within the body.

A person undoubtedly is able, through God's grace and willpower, to resist and triumph. Here, however, we are speaking about the weak-willed person.

A person may sometimes resort to practicing some of these habits to run away from another thought preoccupying his mind, or to run away from a problem or a matter worrying him. If a person has a problem at work, for example, and he thinks a great deal about this matter and cannot get rid of thinking about it, he then sits before the TV; and consequently, a habit is formed for him, that is, to run away to the TV when he has a problem preoccupying his mind and causing him distress. Therefore, thinking about this behavior and submitting to it control a person's life, despite his understanding that this habit harms his social relationships; or it affects his remembrance of his lessons if he is a student; or it is at the expense of his performance at work because he might stay up late at night and go to work exhausted and tired; or it affects his health because he does not get enough sleep.

A person may feel completely powerless before the dominion of this behavior that is causing him harm, and so he does the evil that he does not want to do. A person may not really desire to practice this behavior, but he feels that he cannot overcome it. One of the most wonderful chapters in the Holy Scripture that speaks about this subject is the seventh chapter of the Epistle to the Romans, which speaks about a person without the grace of Christ. And so St. Paul the Apostle says, "For we know that the law is spiritual, but I am carnal, sold under sin."[1]

"The law is spiritual"—the law God gave to Moses, and gave it to us to keep a person spiritual. "But I"—here he is speaking about a person without the grace of Christ, the person before the era of grace. "I am carnal, sold under sin"—that is, I am led by the lust of the flesh. And this presents a description of the person who is subject to a particular habit.

We know that St. Paul the Apostle distinguished between three types of people:

1. The carnal person.

---

1   Romans 7:14.

2. The natural person.

3. The spiritual person.

The carnal person is the one who is under the dominion of the body. For the body controls him. And this applies to most people who are under the bondage of some habits.

As for the natural person, he is not under the dominion of the lusts of the body and its desires, but is under the dominion of his mind; therefore, he is slightly better than the carnal person. This person might say that he will not take drugs or drink alcohol because these things affect his health. By this, he is following the general rules of morality and propriety. This person has high morality; the Apostle, however, says that "the natural man does not receive the things of the Spirit of God,"[2] and consequently, he is lower than the spiritual person.

The spiritual person, however, is the one led by the Holy Spirit, of whom St. Paul the Apostle said that he "judges all things, yet he himself is rightly judged by no one."[3]

St. Paul the Apostle speaks about the person before grace, and says, "I am carnal, sold under sin,"[4] that is, sold to sin, which is [exactly] what we say in the Divine Liturgy, "[He] was incarnate and became man.... [He] gave Himself up unto death, which reigned over us,

---

2   1 Corinthians 2:14.

3   1 Corinthians 2:15.

4   Romans 7:14.

whereby we were bound and sold on account of our sins."

The Apostle continues, saying, "For what I am doing, I do not understand. For what I will to do, that I do not practice; but what I hate, that I do."[5] All those who have an addiction to habits feel that these verses perfectly express the conflict present within them, for they do what they hate, and do not do what they want. The will is present, and they do want to get rid of these habits, but they do what they hate.

"If, then, I do what I will not to do, I agree with the law that it is good."[6] This is because my will is in harmony with the commandment. For the commandment that God gave me is good. The Apostle continues, saying, "But now, it is no longer I who do it, but sin that dwells in me."[7] This is the reason behind my doing what I hate: It is the sin that dwells in me. But by accepting the grace of Christ, the person can control the lusts of his body.

"For I know that in me (that is, in my flesh) nothing good dwells; for to will is present with me, but how to perform what is good I do not find."[8] My weakness is the reason because I am a carnal man, subject to the lusts of the flesh; the Son has not [yet] freed me.

---

5   Romans 7:15.
6   Romans 7:16.
7   Romans 7:17.
8   Romans 7:18.

"For the good that I will to do, I do not do; but the evil I will not to do, that I practice. Now if I do what I will not to do, it is no longer I who do it, but sin that dwells in me. I find then a law, that evil is present with me, the one who wills to do good."[9] Every time I attempt to be victorious, I find evil present before me.

"For I delight in the law of God according to the inward man."[10] I am joyful about God's commandment and do want to carry it out, because my spirit is created in God's image. "But I see another law in my members, warring against the law of my mind, and bringing me into captivity to the law of sin which is in my members. O wretched man that I am! Who will deliver me from this body of death?"[11]

St. Paul the Apostle, nevertheless, immediately remembers the grace of Christ, and says, "I thank God—through Jesus Christ our Lord! So then, with the mind I myself serve the law of God, but with the flesh the law of sin."[12]

As we will speak later, there are means through which a person can be victorious. And these means we call "the means of grace," like prayer, fasting, reading the Holy Scripture, practicing the Church Mysteries such as Confession and Communion. All these are channels that bring us to the grace of our Lord.

---

9   Romans 7:19–21.
10   Romans 7:22.
11   Romans 7:23–24.
12   Romans 7:25.

We sometimes find that the person who is addicted may not have the ability to control this behavior. A person, for example, who has an eating disorder, eats huge amounts despite not wanting to do that. For example, he might want to eat one piece of chocolate, but he brings the box and eats all of it, because he cannot stop eating. He has lost the ability to control this behavior. For by this, he has entered the sphere of what is called compensative behavior. When the person has finished eating the contents of the box, and then the pleasure accompanying this behavior has come to an end, then he has the feeling of guilt, restlessness, sadness, anxiety, and depression.

In some cases, the brain builds a wall against this harmful behavior, preventing the person from remembering this behavior. And this is a type of defense mechanism, because if he remembers this harmful behavior that he did, then this remembrance can make him go into feelings of restlessness, sadness, and depression. The person who is addicted to gambling, for example, his mind completely forgets what he has lost at the gambling table.

At other times, the person tries to conceal these behaviors from others, and so we find him doing these in secret and not declaring them. For example, those who have compulsive shopping habits lose great amounts and purchase many things they do not want to purchase. There might be someone, for example, who wants to buy a belt, but in the end, he comes back having bought three shirts, five pants, and three pairs of shoes, also. And so he begins to conceal this behavior from others because he feels ashamed of his behavior.

Those who are addicted usually suffer from low self-esteem and lack of self-confidence, because they feel that they are a failure with respect to self-control, not being able to control their behavior. This makes some addicts suffer from clinical depression, and they need a specialist for treatment.

When the life history of some addicts was studied, it was noted that they had suffered from some kinds of abuse in their childhood, or that they had grown up in families in which fights and abuse abounded, and so they resorted to addiction to look for pleasure that would take them away from the problems present in the family.

2

Elements of Addiction

To be able to differentiate between addiction and a [mere] habit, there must be six elements to addiction.

1. The presence of something that a person desires or is fascinated by out of curiosity. And this thing may be a habit, an activity, a behavior, a relationship, or anything else.

A young man who wants to experience [smoking] a cigarette does not have a desire for nicotine, but rather he feels that if he began to smoke cigarettes, this would be a kind of manliness. And so this matter fascinated him out of curiosity, but when he began smoking cigarettes, his body became dependent on nicotine, and then a desire for smoking cigarettes arose in him. And what is said about cigarettes applies also to all kinds of drugs or any activity or behavior. For there might be an addiction to a relationship, which would explain what is called "love addiction."

2. This thing has dominion over a person's thinking, which forcefully impels him to fulfill this desire. And so this desire has dominion over him, which is called "obsessive compulsive behavior." The brain is preoccupied with this thing and continues to think about it incessantly.

3. The person begins to be accustomed to a particular behavior to fulfill this desire. He carries this behavior out of his will in the beginning, and he repeats it to satisfy this desire and to get a feeling of pleasure. The first cigarette a man smokes by his will, and this is repeated also with the second and third, and then he repeats it to satisfy his desire and to get a feeling of pleasure.

4. Gradually, the person feels that he has lost control over this behavior, and he carries it out against his will as though he had been robbed of his will. And if he tried to stop it, he would fail; and if he succeeded temporarily in controlling it, he would go back and repeat it once and many times again. With the repetition of the behavior time and again, dependence happens; that is, there is a physical dependence, or a physical and psychological dependence. This means that the body depends on this substance, and psychologically, the person also begins to depend on this behavior.

5. A sort of dependence on this behavior is formed for this person, to satisfy the desire present within him, and as we said in the previous point, this dependence is physical and psychological at the same time.

6. Harm and negative consequences arise from the repetition of this behavior. We will address in detail the harm of addiction and its effect on a person's health, on their spiritual and social relationships, and on their financial state, and so on.

3

Causes of Addiction

1. Some researchers believe that there are hereditary factors for addiction. They found that the children whose parents drank alcohol were also likely to become addicted to alcohol. But is this because of the existence of inherited genes? Or is it because the child grew up in this environment and began imitating his parents, and so he drank alcohol and became addicted?

2. Researchers have also discovered that the cause may be the existence of some mental illnesses, because when a person's mental cognizance is sound, for example, he takes sound decisions and understands the danger of drug addiction, but if his mental cognizance is impaired, this might make him addicted to drugs.

3. Curiosity is one of the causes of addiction. Many children have curiosity. They want to know why people buy cigarettes, and so they desire to try it because they think that it is an expression of manliness. This is what

usually happens with addiction to drugs. Scientists say that the sooner a person begins using these substances or becomes subject to these habits, the more difficult it becomes for him to get rid of them and the more difficult the treatment is than if the person begins at an advanced age.

4.   Another cause of addiction is the negative influence of friendships or the social environment. We might find that a child in school or university may be pressured by his friends to smoke a cigarette like them or to take drugs as they do. Undoubtedly, extreme carelessness, neglect in upbringing or the spoiling of a child, and the abundance of money may lead the child to fall into the trap of addiction. Some children who get a large amount of money try to experience drugs and end up becoming addicts.

5. Suffering from abuse or nervous stress is another cause of addiction. By this, we mean that a person had suffered from abuse in childhood. To be reconciled with himself, he looks for pleasure and pursues anything that can give him this pleasure, and so he falls prey to addiction. And if the child grew up in a home full of problems, in which fights and divisions abounded, then he might end up becoming an addict.

6. Lack of self-control and getting carried away by pleasure are considered among the causes of addiction, and so pleasure becomes a goal for the person instead of being a means. God placed pleasure in some matters so that it may become a means to fulfill them. But if

pleasure became a goal, it would make a person fall into the clutches of addiction. And this is what St. Paul the Apostle said in his epistle to St. Timothy, "But know this, that in the last days perilous times will come: For men will be lovers of themselves, lovers of money, … lovers of pleasure."[13]

In reality, three matters are at war with people: "lovers of themselves" (humanism), "lovers of money" (materialism), and "lovers of pleasure" (hedonism). These are the three things about which St. John the Apostle said, "For all that is in the world—the lust of the flesh, the lust of the eyes, and the pride of life."[14] The lust of the flesh is the love of pleasure; the lust of the eyes is the love of money; and the pride of life is the love of oneself, that is, the ego and pride.

And these three wars are the ones through which the devil fought the Lord Christ in the temptation on the mount. When he said to Him, "Command that these stones become bread," this is the lust of the flesh; when he said, "All these kingdoms I will give You if You will fall down and worship me," this is the love of money or the lust of the eyes; when he said, "Throw Yourself down from the pinnacle of the temple and the angels will bear You up in their hands," this is pride and the ego.

Therefore, lack of self-control and getting carried away by pleasure might make the person all the more a

---

13   2 Timothy 3:1–2, 4.
14   1 John 2:16.

target for addiction. For example, a person eats and is full, but because of pleasure, he continues to eat more. He is practicing a harmful behavior that might make him fall into an addiction to eating (eating disorder).

4

Computer Addiction

Addiction to drugs, to alcohol, and to other things might be far from us, and most of us, if not all, might not suffer from it. Unfortunately, computer addiction, however, began to spread widely among people. Therefore, we find some people, if not the great majority of them, cannot disconnect from computers or the means of modern technology in general. We might find, for example, some children using their phones and sending text messages to each other during the Divine Liturgy. They cannot patiently endure until they have finished praying the Liturgy, and so they pick up their phones to check the messages they have received. This matter, of course, is not befitting of the honor of the Liturgy, from the spiritual viewpoint.

For this reason, we will address in detail the subject of computer addiction, which is widespread nowadays.

1. Computer addiction is the compulsory or coercive use of computers for long periods of time at the expense of other duties, or at the expense of family or social relationships, or even at the expense of personal rest. For example, a student might leave studying and sit in front of his computer, giving the impression to his parents that he is doing his homework on the computer; or an employee, instead of finishing the project he was assigned at work, sits in front of a computer and might play games on it.

It has become evident that computer addiction is currently one of the main causes of divorce, because the husband does not pay attention to his wife but rather sits in front of a computer all day long, or he might not go out to meet his friends even at family gatherings, because he has become addicted to the computer.

2. A person usually spends his time in front of a computer either to play some video games, or to spend time on social media, or to jump from one website to another, or to watch videos on YouTube, or to watch movies one after another, or to shop online. And this might make him become addicted to bad websites on the internet.

3. There are symptoms of computer addiction, of which are the following.

First, a person finds himself using the computer for longer intervals than he had intended. For example, he sits on the computer with the intention of spending half an hour, but finds that he has continued for four hours. As St. Paul the Apostle said, "For to will is present with me, but how to perform what is good I do not find."[15] Therefore, he cannot control the time, and so he continues for many hours unaware.

Second, one of the symptoms is that the person tries to reduce the time he spends on the computer but fails. This failure means that this habit or this behavior has taken control of him. He does not want to spend all this time on the computer, but continues in spite of himself, and he is robbed of his will and becomes under the dominion of this behavior.

Third, constantly thinking about the computer and the pressing desire to seize any opportunity to sit in front of it are also of the symptoms of computer addiction. If the person had to do something, he would soon think about the time when he would go home to sit on the computer to finish a game he had started or to browse social media. Therefore, we find that no sooner does he come home than he sits on the computer for a long time, and this may be to the detriment of his daily duties and studying, and so on.

Fourth, concealing the true number of hours a person spends on the computer from his family and friends is a symptom of addiction. For example, a child sits on the computer until four in the morning, and when asked about the time he went to sleep the day before, he would answer, "After you went to sleep, I

---

15   Romans 7:18.

stayed up for half an hour and then went to sleep." By that, he begins to conceal the time because he cannot control it, all the while he knows that the length of time he had spent on the computer was wrong. For this reason, he cannot confront them with the truth. Therefore, concealing the number of hours a person spends on the computer is a symptom of addiction.

Fifth, one of the consequences resulting from the long time a person spends on the computer is that he cannot fulfill the other life duties. And so he might be dismissed from his job because his superior finds out that he wastes work time on the computer and does not accomplish the work he is assigned.

Six, despite the harm that a person suffers as a consequence of the long time he spends on the computer, he becomes weak-willed and cannot make the decision to stop using the computer, and consequently, serious problems might arise, affecting his family and work.

The Harm of Computer Addiction

There is much harm resulting from computer addiction, including:

1. Social Isolation: that is, a person isolates himself from society, and so he stays away from his friends and family because of his preoccupation with the computer. And even during the time that he spends with them, his mind is preoccupied with the computer and is

scattered, because he is thinking about the things he was doing on the computer, and consequently, he is unable to communicate well with them.

2. Computer addiction affects a person emotionally, because he emotionally interacts with an imaginary world, fictitious and untrue. It is marvelous that the Holy Scripture has warned us against this imaginary world before there were computers, where St. John says, "Having many things to write to you, I did not wish to do so with paper and ink; but I hope to come to you and speak face to face, that our joy may be full."[16] St. John understood the importance of personal communication, person to person: "I did not wish to do so with paper and ink, but I desire to communicate with you personally, person to person, and this matter leads to joy." If St. John had lived until now and had seen how people communicate through text messages, I do not know what he would have said.

And he said the same thing in his third epistle written to Gaius, "I had many things to write, but I do not wish to write to you with pen and ink; but I hope to see you shortly, and we shall speak face to face."[17] We need to reexamine our use of emails and text messages, and to use them in a healthy manner.

3. Computer addiction might lead the person to be tempted to go to evil, immoral, and inappropriate websites, which would lead to another kind of addiction

---

16   2 John 1:12.
17   3 John 1:13-14.

to these sites, and to the defilement and distortion of a person's mind, which would also have repercussions on his family life and social relationships.

4. The person who has become accustomed to communicating with others through the computer finds it difficult to communicate in person with them. He can express himself well through emails, but when he speaks with others face to face, he does not know how to communicate with them.

5. Computer addiction might lead to some health and physical problems with the hands, back, and eyes. Staying up late on the computer for long periods of time and not getting enough sleep have negative effects on a person's nervous and immune systems.

6. Computer addiction might deprive a person, who was accustomed to practicing physical activities like walking and other sports, from practicing these activities, which might expose him to obesity because he sits in front of the computer without moving for many hours.

7. Computer addiction might also lead a person to be dismissed from his job as a consequence of his spending most of his work time playing computer games or visiting websites. This would result in poor performance at work and a lack of commitment to deadlines because he stays up on the computer.

8. One of the most recent statistics has proven that computer addiction has become one of the main causes of marriage failure and divorce.

5

Addiction from the Spiritual Perspective

Our teacher, St. Paul the Apostle, says, "All things are lawful for me, but all things are not helpful. All things are lawful for me, but I will not be brought under the power of any."[18] And because addiction is the habit's exercise of power over a person, the spiritual person who is a child of God will not be brought under the power of anything.

Therefore, the children of God, who have received the new nature in Baptism, in whom the Holy Spirit dwells through the Myron, who have united with Christ through Church Mysteries (Repentance, Confession, and Communion), who have lived for God, and in whom God lives—these should not be subject to, or under the dominion of, anything or

---

18   1 Corinthians 6:12.

any desire. For they have tasted the meaning of true freedom: "If the Son makes you free, you shall be free indeed."[19]

Therefore, after St. Paul the Apostle wrote about this struggle that is the object of inquiry of many people, he said about himself, saying, "But I am carnal, sold under sin."[20] But thanks be to the Lord Jesus, because He died on the cross, freed me, and gave me His grace through the second birth in Baptism, through the indwelling of the Holy Spirit in me, and through Church Mysteries. And this new man, then, is not in subjection to any habit, nor is he under the dominion of anything or any desire.

Among the fruit of the Spirit mentioned in the epistle to the Galatians, we find that the last fruit of the series of the nine fruit of the Spirit is self-control.[21] And since we are still in this world, we are exposed to the temptations of sin. But the person who has become filled with the Holy Spirit and has borne the fruit of self-control in his life, nothing will have dominion over him, because he knows how to restrain and to control himself well.

Temptations might come from the world, from the devil, or from the lusts of the flesh, but the Holy Spirit who dwells in us grants the power to reject these temptations and resist them.

---

19   John 8:36.
20   Romans 7:14.
21   See Galatians 5:23.

Among the verses that are very comforting on the subject of addiction is the verse mentioned in the first epistle to the Corinthians. Before mentioning the verse, it is worth noting that the Arabic word *"tajruba"* has two meanings: it may mean hardship as in the English word "trial," or it may mean the enticement of sin as in the English word "temptation." Both "trial" and "temptation" are translated to the same Arabic word *"tajruba,"* leading to improper understanding. For example, St. James says in his epistle, "My brethren, count it all joy when you fall into various trials [*tajārub*],"[22] and then he says, "Let no one say when he is tempted [*juriba*], 'I am tempted [*ujarab*] by God'; for God cannot be tempted [*mujarab*] by evil, nor does He Himself tempt [*ujarib*] anyone. But each one is tempted [*ujarrab*] when he is drawn away by his own desires and enticed."[23] In the former verse, when a person enters into trials, he should count it all joy, because trials produce patience, which will help in building up his personality and spiritual life. As for the latter verse, the word means temptation or the enticement of sin.

St. Paul says in his first epistle to the Corinthians, "No temptation has overtaken you except such as is common to man; but God is faithful, who will not allow you to be tempted beyond what you are able, but with the temptation will also make the way of

---

22   James 1:2.
23   James 1:13-14.

escape, that you may be able to bear it."[24] That is, the temptation of sin that all of us encounter is within the limits of human capabilities, and this is the meaning of "common to men." God does not allow us to be exposed to the temptations of sin that are beyond our abilities; therefore, the temptations of the world, the body, or the devil are within human capabilities, and by the grace of the Lord, a person is able to overcome them. For this reason, he said, "But with the temptation will also make the way of escape, that you may be able to bear it." That is, there is a way out, the help, and the power that God bestows. Also, the work of the Holy Spirit in the life of a person enables him to resist addiction.

Nevertheless, the Christian must be very careful from the start so that he may not practice a negative behavior or try a substance, and so he may not fall into the bondage of addiction. For an ounce of prevention is worth a pound of cure.

And if some have fallen captive to addiction or some bad habits, they should not fall into despair, for there is always a very high hope of healing, because the Lord Christ has promised to free us: "Therefore if the Son makes you free, you shall be free indeed."[25]

Desire is the origin and beginning of numerous sins. Adultery first begins by the lust of the flesh;

---

24   1 Corinthians 10:13.
25   John 8:36.

stealing begins by the desire for possessing or the desire for money; lying begins by the desire to justify oneself or to scheme something; murder begins by the desire for revenge or by another desire leading to it. Therefore, if a person wages war against his sinful desires and emerges victorious over them, then he will have become victorious over numerous sins.

Pope Shenouda III

6

Symptoms of Addiction

We have already spoken about the general symptoms of addiction that are manifested in the person who is addicted. But we will now speak about the symptoms that parents can discover in their children, which may enable them to confirm that their child has actually become addicted or that he is on his way to becoming addicted. There are many indications, some of which are the following.

1. Negligence in the Daily Responsibilities Such as Studying and Work. The child's school grades begin to drop after he was outstanding; or the child, who has a job, stops going to work regularly; or he runs away and does not go to work; and so on.

2. Extreme Fluctuations in Mood. On one occasion, he is extremely happy, and on another, he is extremely sad. And there is no explanation for these acute fluctuations, nor are they related to the surrounding circumstances.

3. Sleeping a Great Deal, or Little, or Rarely. The parents discover that their child sleeps a great deal. If he were driving a car, for example, when he stops at the red light, he would fall asleep; or upon arrival at home, as soon as the car is parked, he would fall asleep in it before coming out of it. Or he might abnormally sleep while sitting at his desk. Or he might sleep very little or rarely.

4. Sudden Change in Energy. Sometimes he is very energetic, while at other times he is lethargic, very tired, and exhausted, unable to do anything.

5. Abnormal Weight Loss or Constant Weight Gain.

6. Instability or Unsteadiness of Health. He appears tired or exhausted, his health unstable.

7. The pupil of the eye might be smaller or larger than the normal size.

8. Lying. The child begins to lie because he wants to cover up his addiction. And it is easy to detect his lying.

9. Secrecy. The child begins to surround his actions with secrecy, and he ensures concealment so that his addiction is not discovered.

10. Stealing. The child might resort to stealing because addiction demands a large amount of money, as those addicted to narcotics do.

11. Money. We might find that the child suddenly has a huge amount of money from an unknown source, or he might be in dire need of money. This is a matter that represents a grave danger: that the child may turn into a small drug dealer. He may resort to this to make money, by which he can buy the drugs he is addicted to. Therefore, he might accumulate a huge amount of money from an unknown source.

Or he might be in dire need of money. And this need might make him a violent person, to the extent that he may assault his father or mother to get the money necessary to buy the drugs that his body seeks.

12. Changing His Friends and Making Suspicious Phone Calls. The child begins to befriend new children whose behavior is strange to that of the children of God. And he might shroud his phone calls with secrecy, because it is possible that through them he is making transactions to buy or sell.

13. Going out Frequently from the House. This is to unknown places with an intense feeling of the necessity to go out. Sometimes he gives the parents the feeling that he has to go instantly out, because if he did not go out, a serious problem would take place.

14. Changing the Kind of Friends He Keeps.

15. Discovering the Items Needed for Addiction or Discovering the Drugs Themselves. The parents might discover the things their son uses to take drugs or the drugs themselves in his pockets, his drawer, his desk, or his bag.

There is finally a point of paramount importance: that is, the presence of these symptoms does not mean that your son is an addict, for there might be many other causes for these symptoms; therefore, do not judge hastily if you discover some of these symptoms. Likewise, do not be so naive, however, as to be deceived by your son, believing that he does not use drugs. The early discovery of addiction in children who are addicted to drugs makes their treatment much easier than if they had been addicted for a long time before we began treating them.

The aforementioned are general symptoms of addiction. There are, however, specific symptoms for every kind of drug, for the symptoms of a particular narcotic are different from the symptoms of another. There are also specific symptoms for behavioral addiction, for the behavior of the person addicted to eating is different from the behavior of the one addicted to shopping, and so on.

Four things protect young people from bad thoughts: reading the Holy Scriptures, casting laziness away, rising up in the night for prayer, and being endued with humility always.

St. Moses the Strong

7

Treatment of Addiction

It is necessary to stress at the beginning that there is a part that needs a specialist in the addiction treatment, which is called "detoxification," especially for those who abuse substances like narcotics and drugs. This treatment is based on the withdrawal of the narcotic substance from the body. This is not our area of speech, for there are specialists for it. Rather, we will focus on the treatment for addiction in general, and the behavioral addiction specifically; that is, habit addictions, because a person, with God's help, can overcome them without needing to go to a psychiatrist. This is different from substance abuse, because this addiction needs an addiction treatment center and a rehabilitation center.

Many people who are addicted refuse treatment because they feel that they have no problem. They believe that they can stop practicing this addictive behavior at any time they wish. Also, some of them are unwilling to make an effort to get rid of this addiction, although making an effort is an essential condition of getting rid of the addiction.

Some refuse treatment because they do not have the willingness to get rid of addiction for the sake of the pleasure resulting from it. The person who is addicted enjoys the transitory pleasure that they obtain from addiction. They also enjoy the way of life they are living.

Those who are addicted refuse treatment also because of their feelings of failure and despair of the possibility of getting rid of their addiction, and consequently, they give in to it. For this reason, they refuse any attempt at treatment because they have tried before but have failed, and have become persuaded that there is no point in their trying.

Some of them do not want to be treated because they do not want to live a normal life with all that it demands of duties and responsibilities, while they do not want to take responsibility.

Specialists in the treatment of addiction discovered that sometimes the person who is addicted does not seek treatment except when he has hit the bottom. If the addiction has begun to cause him dreadful and deep-rooted problems, then he seeks treatment. And this is what happened with the prodigal son, who decided to return to his father's house when he hit the bottom. For he had no money and began to be in need, and he would desire to eat of the pods of the swine, and yet no one gave him anything. And here he began to come to himself and say, "I will arise and go to my father."[26] And we may wonder about this story: If the father knew the news about his son, his need and his inability to get even the pods which the swine ate, and he had compassion on him and said, "I will send him some food and money, so that he may know that I love him," and so he indeed sent him food and money, would this lead to the return of the son? Undoubtedly no. And yet this is what we do, unfortunately. Many parents intervene, with the motive of love, to rescue their children from the problems they have fallen into because of addiction, and they are unaware that this rescuing will make their children persist all the more in addiction.

Therefore, it is sometimes advised that in case of refusal to be treated, to leave the children to suffer from the problems of addiction, and this will speed up their complete descent to the bottom, and then they will seek treatment for this dangerous illness.

At the same time, the Church and the family, however, must have their eyes on her addicted child so that she can rescue him at the appropriate time. We do not mean by "leaving him" that he should be kicked out of the house, but that we should let him deal with the problem he is suffering from; nevertheless, we should have our eyes on him, and we should follow up with him and ask about him, without intervening

---

26   Luke 15:18.

to save him from the problem. Rather, we should leave him to deal with it until he comes on his own, seeking treatment. And this does not mean that we should deal thus with all cases, but only with the children who refuse treatment.

The many and convincing means must not be unknown to parents and guides, means to which those addicted resort, so that they may conceal their addiction and persuade those around them that they are not addicted.

Treatment varies according to the needs of the person who is addicted, that is, according to the stage he has reached in his addiction and according to the type of his addiction. There are many types of treatment, including the following:

1. Detoxification. The word "toxins" means toxic compounds. What is meant by this treatment is the removal of the toxic compounds from the human body resulting from alcohol and narcotics. Here, the person who is addicted must enter an addiction treatment center and submit to a particular treatment program that makes the body completely eliminate the toxic compounds of the narcotics that have entered it.

2. One-on-One Therapy. The method of one-on-one treatment is suitable for some people, and so the person who is addicted sits with a counselor or therapist.

3. Group Therapy. Group therapy suits others through support groups. One of the distinguishing features of this method is that it offers support and aid. The person who is addicted needs love because he has low self-esteem, feels depressed, and has feelings of failure and despair. Therefore, the more others embrace him with love and offer him encouragement, the greater power this gives him to overcome addiction. Declaring the love of God for him is very important, of course. It is necessary for him to feel the divine love.

4. Rehab Centers. Some people who are addicted are treated in specialized centers. For they do not need a treatment to remove the toxins from their bodies, but they are rather placed in rehabilitation centers that keep them away from the world for a particular period of time until they go back to a normal state, and afterwards they go out into the world.

5. Self-Help Treatment. There is also a self-help treatment method, in which a person treats himself through reading some books or through self-help groups. And this includes the twelve steps that have proved their efficacy in treating many, especially from alcohol addiction.

8

Stages of Recovery from Behavioral Habits & Addiction

For a person to recover from the dominion of a habit or from addiction, he goes through several stages.

1. The Decision-Making. This stage is very important because many who are addicted refuse treatment or do not admit that they have a problem. Therefore, the first stage is that the person who is addicted should make the decision to be treated. And here, the family, Church, and friends have a major role in helping the person who is addicted make this decision, whether by convincing him, or by offering him love, or by trying to help him recognize the harm of addiction and the problems he suffers from; and possibly by using some sort of firmness, to the extent that in some cases the father may obtain a court order to subject his son to treatment against his will.

Some are afraid of this method. Studies, however, have proved that the addicts who were treated or were admitted into centers for rehabilitation and treatment against their will, when they were healed and returned to their normal state, they felt gratitude and thankfulness toward their families because they had rescued them from the clutches of addiction.

2. Determining the Kind of Treatment. The kind of treatment suitable for the person who is addicted must be determined, and more than one method may be used together.

3. The Decision's Implementation. This stage requires a strong support system that satisfies the person and provides love, help, and support, because the struggle here is fierce. For it is the struggle of a slave trying to rebel against his master to obtain his freedom. Addiction is a cruel master, and the addict is a slave whose will has been robbed and is under the cruelty of this master. Therefore, he needs help and support, of course, divine support and the help of the Holy Spirit, and the powerful intercessions of the saints, so that he can break the shackles of slavery and be free.

4. Becoming Accustomed to a New Lifestyle Without Addiction. The addict's lifestyle must be altered; the kind of friends [he associates with] must be altered; the way in which he spends his day must be altered. And his behavior will be altered also, and so will he exchange one habit for another habit, and will be accustomed to a sound and healthy lifestyle away from addiction.

5. Discovering Non-Addictive Means to Overcome the Desire to Go Back to Addiction. In some cases, a relapse might take place, and he might also feel the desire to drink alcohol or take drugs; therefore, there has to be some healthy means that will help him overcome the desire to go back to addiction once again.

6. Perseverance Until the End in the Path of No-Return to Addiction. The person must struggle and persevere so that he may not go back to addiction once again: "But he who endures to the end shall be saved."[27]

The Success of Treatment

The success of the treatment depends on the following:

1. The Willingness of the Addict to Change. Does he act with seriousness, in that he wants to get rid of addiction, and consequently, he accepts and submits to the treatment presented to him? Or does he try to deceive people and fool the doctor?

2. Hope, Perseverance, and Determination. As we have previously said, an addict's refusal to be treated may stem from his feeling of despair, and that there is no use in treatment. Therefore, we need to give him hope, not hope in a person but hope in the Lord Jesus Christ, of whom St. Paul the Apostle said, "[He] who

---

27   Matthew 24:13.

delivered us from so great a death, and does deliver us; in whom we trust that He will still deliver us."[28] So the Lord Jesus Christ delivered us, delivers us, and will deliver us also.

3. The Degree of Addiction. The success of the treatment of addiction depends on the degree of addiction, its duration, the substances abused, and so on.

4. The Health of the Addict. The greater the degree to which health has deteriorated because of addiction, the longer the time it takes to be treated.

5. The Mental and Psychological Condition of the Addict. The addict who is suffering from clinical depression will take longer to be treated. The same also applies to the addict who is suffering from a mental illness. This mental and psychological condition may influence the success of the treatment.

6. The Presence of a Support System. The presence of a support system around the person who is addicted will strengthen them and help them overcome their addiction.

7. The Material and Financial Condition. The person who is addicted needs to stay in an addiction treatment center for extended periods of time, and consequently, they stay away from their job for a long time and have no source of income. The Church, nonprofit organizations, and anti-addiction

---

28   2 Corinthians 1:10.

organizations must play a vital role in helping these people financially, so that they may be able to complete their treatment. The benefit to society after they recover from their addiction will be immense.

9

The Spiritual Treatment

As we have previously said, the treatment of addiction needs a strong support system. And this support comes foremost from a strong spiritual relationship with God. Therefore, the success of treatment is founded principally upon this relationship. If a person neglects the spiritual aspect, they will relapse and return to addiction.

1. Teaching. To persuade the addict of the treatment from the spiritual aspect, I must discuss with him the consequences of addiction and its effect on his relationship with God, on himself, on all those around him. I must also open his eyes to understand that the present pleasure resulting from addiction blinds the person to the real imminent danger. Pleasure blinds the addict, and so he needs a person to enlighten his eyes.

2. Sin Against God. This is a sin that saddens God's heart. For we are the temple of God, and the

Holy Scripture directs to us a severe warning when it says: "Do you not know that you are the temple of God and that the Spirit of God dwells in you? If anyone defiles the temple of God, God will destroy him. For the temple of God is holy, which temple you are."[29] For addiction to substances and habits defiles the temple of God.

3. Sin Against Oneself. This sin brings sadness into a person's heart and affects his health, his social relationships, his job, his future, and his reputation. Some students, for example, lose the scholarships they had been granted because of addiction.

4. Bad Example. This sin is also a bad example to others, and it destroys the addict's relationship with his family. The father who smokes cigarettes, for example, cannot order his children not to smoke cigarettes, for he is a bad example to his children.

And many cases of divorce have happened because of the husband's addiction to gambling. For he might resort to remortgaging his house and selling their possessions. For this reason, the wife leaves him to protect herself.

5. Paying a High Price. It often happens that the price the addict pays for his addiction is extremely high. Many young men ended up in prison because they sold drugs or were addicted, thereby destroying their future.

---

29   1 Corinthians 3:16–17.

6. Facing the Truth and Confession. It is necessary that the person who is addicted faces the truth and confesses his addiction before himself, before God, and before his father of confession, without trying to justify his behavior or deny it. Confession means that a person must bear the responsibility and must not seek excuses.

7. Holding onto Hope and Being Certain of the Ability to be Victorious in the Name of the Lord Christ. The feeling of despair and the spirit of defeatism will not make him enthusiastic about the idea of treatment. The church at Corinth used to suffer from many problems, one of which was a moral problem, like the man who fell into sin with his father's wife; St. Paul the Apostle, however, treated this man and led him to repentance, despite these problems and the diffusion of the stench of sin. And he said a powerful statement, "Now thanks be to God who always leads us in triumph in Christ, and through us diffuses the fragrance of His knowledge in every place."[30]

8. Admitting One's Weakness and Powerlessness, and Seeking Divine Help. A person must feel his powerlessness, admit his weakness, and rely on divine help. St. Paul the Apostle had reached the point of despair and said, "We despaired even of life."[31] He had as though reached the bottom, but he said after that, "That we should not trust in ourselves but in God who

---

30   2 Corinthians 2:14.
31   2 Corinthians 1:8.

raises the dead, who delivered us from so great a death, and does deliver us; in whom we trust that He will still deliver us."[32] Therefore, the addict can overcome if he feels his utter powerlessness and seeks help from God, putting all his trust in Him.

His Holiness Pope Shenouda III says in a poem he wrote, titled "I have Drenched My Bed with My Bitter Tears," "The power is from You, from above, and not from me; so long as You are with me, I will not go back again."

Abba Isaac says, "He who believes that there is another way to repentance, apart from prayer, is deceived by the demons," because by prayer we obtain divine help and grace. Therefore, a person must resort to prayer so that God may grant them the power to overcome.

9. The Word of God and Its Power to Liberate a Person and Purify the Mind. The word of God is more powerful than a two-edged sword.[33] It liberates a person and breaks the bonds of sin. The Lord Jesus Christ said to His disciples, "You are already clean because of the word which I have spoken to you."[34] In the word of God, there is a marvelous power to liberate a person and purify him; therefore, reading the Holy Scripture continually, and spiritual books also, gives the person the victory over sin. As Abba Anthony said, "Frequent reading of the Divine Books enlightens the mind." For

---

32   2 Corinthians 1:9–10.

33   See Hebrews 4:12.

34   John 15:3.

the person who frequently reads the Divine Books and spiritual books, his mind becomes enlightened, and he is liberated from the bondage of thoughts that have dominion over him, which lead him to addiction.

10. Revealing the Thought and Revealing the Sin. The fathers say, "Revealing the sin weakens its power." Many people feel ashamed of confessing their sin, a thing that empowers it and makes it have dominion over them. But whenever a person reveals his thoughts, casting them out and bringing them out to the light of Christ, their power is weakened. And this is the power and beauty of the Mystery of Confession, where a person reveals his sins and his thoughts before the father of confession, who also holds the person accountable, because a big and important part of the success of the addiction treatment depends on the presence of someone who holds the person accountable, strengthens them, and encourages them; and this is what the father of confession does.

11. Fleeing from the Causes of Sin. To get rid of addiction, a person must flee from the causes of sin, as the angels said to Lot, "Escape for your life! Do not look behind you nor stay anywhere in the plain."[35] And as our teacher St. Peter said about Lot, "For that righteous man, dwelling among them, tormented his righteous soul from day to day by seeing and hearing their lawless deeds."[36] If I were to abstain from smoking cigarettes

---

35   Genesis 19:17.

36   2 Peter 2:8.

while my friends smoked, then I would go back once again to smoking. Likewise is the case with respect to drinking alcohol. Therefore, there has to be resistance and struggle, as our teacher St. Paul says, "You have not yet resisted to bloodshed, striving against sin."[37]

When a person is filled with the Holy Spirit, he possesses self-control, and then he possesses the strong will with which he says "No" to the temptation of sin, as Joseph said, "How then can I do this great wickedness, and sin against God?"[38] St. John the Apostle also says, "I have written to you, young men, because you are strong, and the word of God abides in you, and you have overcome the wicked one."[39]

12. Support System. A person must also surround himself with a support system. There are two kinds of support systems: one visible and another invisible. This latter one is the cloud of witnesses surrounding us and also the work of the Holy Spirit in a person's heart. St. Paul the Apostle has spoken about this invisible system, saying, "Therefore we also, since we are surrounded by so great a cloud of witnesses, let us lay aside every weight, and the sin which so easily ensnares us, and let us run with endurance the race that is set before us."[40] For the saints grant us help through their intercessions so that we may overcome sin.

---

37   Hebrews 12:4.
38   Genesis 39:9.
39   1 John 2:14.
40   Hebrews 12:1.

The visible support system is through the Church. For this reason, God did not make us worship Him as individuals only, but made us worship Him as an assembled people. Therefore, we say in the Divine Liturgy, "He made us unto Himself an assembled people,"[41] because assembling in the body of Christ makes us support and strengthen each other. The family, also, as a visible support system, must play a major role in protecting the person who is addicted.

13. Service, Using One's Talents, and Exchanging a Habit for a Habit. When a person uses the talents that God gave him and occupies himself by serving others, he will receive the blessing of service, and his heart will rejoice in the service that he fulfills. As the Lord Jesus Christ said, "And whoever gives one of these little ones only a cup of cold water in the name of a disciple, assuredly, I say to you, he shall by no means lose his reward."[42] It is difficult for the person who serves to go back to the habits he has decided to give up. By this, also, he exchanges bad habits for beautiful habits, serving others and praising God.

Causes of Relapse

So that we may exhaustively treat the subject of addiction, we will take a quick look at the causes of relapse: what makes a person who has overcome a particular behavior or some habit go back once again

---

41   The Divine Liturgy of St. Basil – Holy.

42   Matthew 10:42.

to his addiction. There are many causes, but we can summarize them in the following:

1. Old Friends. If the person surrounds himself again with those who were the main reason for him falling prey to addiction, he might go back once again to addiction.

2. An Environment that Can Cause Someone to Stumble. A person who was addicted to alcohol, for example, who succeeded in recovering from it, if this person works at a pub for selling or consuming alcoholic beverages, he will go back again to his addiction.

3. How Others Treat the Recovering Addict. Another one of the causes of relapse is the treatment of others, especially the family. If family members begin to criticize the person, continually remind him of what has happened to him because of addiction, put him to shame because of his addiction, and compare him with his siblings, it is possible that he would increasingly suffer from low self-esteem and go back to addiction. This is because he feels that addiction gives him transitory pleasure that would get him out of the feeling of low self-esteem.

4. Instability. A person, for example, may return to a home filled with problems, which is never without quarrels, where instability, tension, and nervous stress prevail. All these may make him go back to addiction again.

5. Society's View. Society's view of the person who has recovered from his addiction may also be a cause of relapse. Therefore, St. Paul the Apostle, when he perceived the repentance of the person who had sinned in Corinth, sent an epistle, admonishing the people of Corinth not to treat him in a way that would trouble him. He said to them, "This punishment which was inflicted by the majority is sufficient for such a man, so that, on the contrary, you ought rather to forgive and comfort him, lest perhaps such a one be swallowed up with too much sorrow."[43] He is saying that what happened to him because of his sin was sufficient for him, and they should forgive him and receive him with true love. Then he says a powerful and beautiful statement: "Lest perhaps such a one be swallowed up with too much sorrow." It is necessary for society's view of the person who is healed from addiction to be a view full of love and acceptance. "I say to you that likewise there will be more joy in heaven over one sinner who repents than over ninety-nine just persons who need no repentance."[44]

This may also happen in the Church community. Sometimes, a person who has been freed from the bondage of addiction comes and tries to approach his friends, but you find that people are afraid of him and distance themselves from him. Therefore, they must remember the verse in which St. Paul the Apostle said, "You ought rather to forgive and comfort him.... Therefore I urge you to reaffirm your love to him."[45]

---

43   2 Corinthians 2:6–7.

44   Luke 15:7.

45   2 Corinthians 2:7–8.

6. The Lack of a Good Example. A person, for example, has gotten rid of his addiction, but when he comes back, he finds that the people he is dealing with and emulates also have behavioral and moral problems, and they even have addictions. This makes him relapse and go back to addiction.

7. Neglect of the Spiritual Aspect. A final cause of relapse is the neglect of the spiritual aspect. For the person who began to pray, to go to church, to seek the intercessions of the saints, to confess and receive Communion, and to read the Holy Scripture, and so he overcame his addiction, but then he begins to neglect these means of grace, this person may fall into relapse. Therefore, the persistence in practicing the means of grace is a very important matter.

One final and very important word is that the addict is a person who is sick. He needs to be loved, to be given a helping hand, and to be prayed for, because love is the true treatment for the person who is addicted.

And to our God be glory forever. Amen.

10

Motivating Verses that Help in Overcoming Addiction

"I beseech you therefore, brethren, by the mercies of God, that you present your bodies a living sacrifice, holy, acceptable to God, which is your reasonable service. And do not be conformed to this world, but be transformed by the renewing of your mind, that you may prove what is that good and acceptable and perfect will of God."[46]

"Walk in the Spirit, and you shall not fulfill the lust of the flesh."[47]

"I beg you as sojourners and pilgrims, abstain from fleshly lusts which war against the soul."[48]

---

46   Romans 12:1–2.

47   Galatians 5:16.

48   1 Peter 2:11.

"But now having been set free from sin, and having become slaves of God, you have your fruit to holiness, and the end, everlasting life."[49]

"Do not present your members as instruments of unrighteousness to sin, but present yourselves to God as being alive from the dead, and your members as instruments of righteousness to God."[50]

"Add to your faith virtue, to virtue knowledge, to knowledge self-control, to self-control perseverance, to perseverance godliness, to godliness brotherly kindness, and to brotherly kindness love."[51]

"But solid food belongs to those who are of full age, that is, those who by reason of use have their senses exercised to discern both good and evil."[52]

49   Romans 6:22.

50   Romans 6:13.

51   2 Peter 1:5–7.

52   Hebrews 5:14.

www.ingramcontent.com/pod-product-compliance
Lightning Source LLC
Chambersburg PA
CBHW021141130726
47988CB00003B/1406